ENDORSEMENTS

"I encourage you to steal away with *Jesus, Coffee and Prayer*. Minister Nakita Davis has written a wonderfully concise fourteen-day devotional that encourages us to meditate on what it means to walk with God. It is the perfect book for a sabbatical that leaves you renewed, reflective, and revived. Within these pages, Nakita gets to the core of how an attitude of prayer and humility can significantly enhance your spiritual well-being. You will be blessed!"

~ Min. K.D. Johnson, President,
Engage Ministers & Psalmists Alliance,
K.D. Johnson Ministries,
author of *God's Got a Method: Biblical Instruction for Victorious Christian Living*

"There is a plethora of cookie-cutter, seemingly perfect devotionals that we've all read. I *love* how *Jesus, Coffee, and Prayer* (Attitude of Gratitude series) is not only easy to digest, but also filled with real-life, day-to-day struggles that we all face. It's a perfect read to go along with your daily one-on-one time with our Lord and Savior."

~ Keisha Michelle Ministries

"I *love* this book! I wish it was longer. Fourteen days isn't enough. I wanted more. Minister Nakita Davis is a wonderful writer. She makes clear points that are relatable and to the point. This devotional is written well and clearly *anointed!*"

~ Angela Anagho
wife and stay-at-home mother of four

JESUS, COFFEE, AND PRAYER

ATTITUDE OF GRATITUDE
SERIES

NAKITA DAVIS

JESUS, COFFEE, AND PRAYER
Copyright © 2018 by Nakita Davis.

All rights reserved. No part of this publication may be reproduced, distributed or transmitted in any form or by any means, including photocopying, recording, or other electronic or mechanical methods, without the prior written permission of the publisher, except in the case of brief quotations embodied in critical reviews and certain other noncommercial uses permitted by copyright law. For permission requests, write to the author at the e-mail address below.

Jesuscoffeeandprayer@gmail.com

Unless otherwise indicated, all Scripture taken from the HOLY BIBLE, NEW INTERNATIONAL VERSION®. NIV®. Copyright © 1973, 1978, 1984 by International Bible Society. Used by permission of Zondervan. All rights reserved worldwide.

All Scripture quotations marked NKJV are taken from the New King James Version®. Copyright © 1982 by Thomas Nelson. Used by permission. All rights reserved.

Editing and typesetting: Sally Hanan of Inksnatcher.com
Cover design: PixelStudio

Ordering Information:
Quantity sales. Special discounts are available on quantity purchases by corporations, associations, and others. For details, contact the author at the e-mail address above.

Jesus, Coffee, and Prayer/Nakita Davis
ISBN 978-0999818800

To my mother, Luetta Williams. You will always be in my heart and I know that you are smiling down from heaven! I thank Jesus for allowing you to be the best example of Christ that I have ever known. Your countless prayers, your praise, your hardships, and your selfless acts were not in vain. I am the woman in Christ, wife, and mother of two because of the values Jesus instilled in me through you! I love you, Momma, and know that I will see you again.

CONTENTS

Day 1 You Are Not Alone 1
Day 2 Fix Your Focus 9
Day 3 God's Perfect Timing 15
Day 4 Be Still 23
Day 5 Outshine Pain 29
Day 6 Last Place Wins 35
Day 7 Sitting on a Million 43
Day 8 Messy Praise 49
Day 9 Missing the Mark 55
Day 10 Better or Bitter 63
Day 11 It's All Good 71
Day 12 In the End 79
Day 13 Create Space 85
Day 14 Wait in Hope 93

About the Author 101
A Moment with the Author 103
Sneak Peek Book Sequel 107

Preface

First and foremost, I have to give honor to my creator, provider, savior, Father, and friend, Jesus Christ. Without him, nothing is possible, and with him, all things are possible! As I become a more mature Christian, striving to live on every word of God; the Lord has helped me realize that my joy and my blessed state of mind have very little to do with my day-to-day emotions and more to do about his goodness. Regardless of the situation, regardless of the outcome—my expectations being exceeded or not met—my attitude should be one of gratitude and one praiseworthy to the almighty King!

Jesus, Coffee, and Prayer, is a spiritual collection of Scripture, perspective, prayer, and more. In this specific series, an attitude of gratitude will be conveyed in each blessed devotional! I need a whole lot of Jesus, a little bit of coffee, and much-needed prayer!

As you embrace our journey, know that Jesus is the Word and Scripture, coffee refers to my perspective, and the *prayer* is the *prayer*. So join me as we explore gratitude—a feeling of thankfulness and appreciation, for the highest King!

And remember, my sisters and brothers, real gratitude is never silent. By the end of our journey, I challenge you to take action in a real and tangible way! Now you may say that's easier said than done! And I would say you're absolutely right. That's why I believe the Lord has placed on my heart the desire to share exactly how to have an attitude of gratitude with my friends, brothers and sisters, and believers in Christ.

Philippians 4:8 clearly tells us to focus on "whatever is true, whatever is noble, whatever is right, whatever is pure, whatever is lovely, whatever is admirable—if anything is excellent or praiseworthy."

My past experience has been similar to many of yours. Instead of showing an attitude of gratitude, appreciation, and positivity for the day and the blessings given, I, too, have been guilty of grumbling and complaining, of mumbling through the day and skipping the beauty of God's glory. But God, through much needed prayer, devotion, and deliberate actions taken to grow my relationship with Christ, has enabled me to see a brighter perspective—a perspective I hope to share with you on your own journey to sincere gratitude. I pray that this devotional is the fundamental stepping stone for you to break the chains of negativity, the spirit of complaint, and the destruction that you may unknowingly be speaking over your life.

Proverbs 18:21 tells us "The tongue has the power of life and death, and those who love it will eat its fruit." I pray that you are fruitful and multiply in his Word.

So lean in, open your Bible app, grab your favorite cup of joe, and get ready for the Holy Spirit to shift your atmosphere.

Love,

Nakita

OPENING PRAYER

Heavenly Father,

As your faithful servant, I come to you with praise and thanksgiving on my lips. You are the great I am and all glory belongs to you, dear Lord. If I had a thousand tongues, I couldn't thank you enough. You are the air I breathe and the words I write. I love you, Jesus, and I recognize all of this—this book, the words written, the readers, and the listeners are all because of you!

My earnest prayer is that you bless, exceedingly and abundantly, every reader and every person with the desire to read your devotionals and walk with an attitude of gratitude. I pray that your people would be receptive to your words, your will, and your way. I pray that I have made you proud by being obedient to the calling you have placed over my life. I don't pray for fame or fortune but for wisdom, discernment, and spiritual growth. I pray that your people will use this book to break free from negativity and the spirit of complaint in their hearts. Be so gracious, Lord, as to soften the hearts of your people, so they may humble themselves before your mighty hand.

And at the sound of my voice, I command the enemy to release every bondage, every yoke, every shackle, and every generational curse held on your people! Right now, in the mighty name of Jesus, I speak life! And if I have found favor in your eyes, dear Lord, allow these things to come to pass.

In Jesus's name I pray; in God's name I ask, amen

DAY 1

YOU ARE NOT ALONE

JESUS

DEUTERONOMY 31:6

Be strong and courageous. Do not be afraid or terrified because of them, for the Lord your God goes with you; he will never leave you or forsake you.

Coffee

When you're going through a test, trial, or tribulation, the first thing the enemy wants you to feel is abandonment, fear, and separation from Jesus Christ. He will attempt to tell you lies—Where is God when you need him, why would he allow you to go through this (again), and doesn't he care for you? to name a few. In contrast to Satan's ill attempts to cause us despair, we, as Christians, must know that our Lord is with us at all times. When the world seems to push us away, the love of Jesus Christ is drawing us nearer to the cross.

As I encourage you, I encourage myself. This devotional comes at a time of rapid change and growth in my personal life. As I finish out my second trimester with my second child (my husband's and my first son), I received news of a failing glucose test. This is a very important test taken to detect potential diabetes. These results were virtually identical to the results I received with my first child almost ten years ago. Back then, I was prediabetic with high blood pressure and in serious jeopardy of preeclampsia. *But* God!

Although gestational diabetes is a real issue and will be addressed with the appropriate medical team, I count it *all joy!* Whereas the enemy wants me to believe Here you go *again,* God wants me to know, I delivered you once and I am faithful to *do it again!* You see, the situation may be similar, but my perspective is reflective of God's goodness, faithfulness, and favor over my life and my child's life! I see this as an opportunity to give God a praise break before and during the storm! I no longer have to wait to see if I *win!* When Jesus died on the cross, he gave *me* and *you* the victory!

What the enemy means for my bad, God means for my good! And this, too, will be a testimony of his grace, mercy, and hedge of protection over his children! You see, ten years ago, Jesus Christ had already been accepted into my life, but I didn't have a relationship with the King. Now I have the honor and privilege of knowing him more and more, day by day, through his living, breathing Word, his grace and mercy, and his love for me!

When I was thirsty, the Lord literally gave me something to drink vicariously through his people. But now that I know the Lord and love him with all my heart and all that is within me, he has given me a drink from the well that never runs dry!

So be of good cheer and know Jesus is with you, even as you stand in the midst of your test. Keep your focus on him and praise him toward your victory. Your praise breaks chains and confuses the enemy!

Prayer

> Heavenly Father, I come to you again saying *Thank you!* Your grace and mercy endure on and on! You are all that is lovely, all that is noble and good in my life! I thank you in

advance for the hardships I must endure for your glory. Just like Paul, I consider my current sufferings not worthy when compared to your glory that will reveal itself within me! I trust you, Lord, in the ordinary times and the extraordinary times, in the good times, the bad times, and the times in-between. No matter the circumstance, Lord, create in me a spirit of victory, a boldness like Joshua's, and a song of praise on my lips like David's! As I encourage myself, allow me to encourage others with the zeal of you! I will reflect on your goodness and your faithfulness all the days of my life, and to the very ends of the earth!

In Jesus's name I pray; in God's name I ask, amen.

Attitude of Gratitude

On the next page, and every day, I will ask you to journal by writing down your attitude of gratitude statements.

When you list an attitude of gratitude statement, you are writing down who or what you are grateful for on that day, specifically, and why.

Example: I am grateful for the financial resource you have provided, Jesus, on this day, with which I am able to fill up my refrigerator, freezer, and cabinets with food for my growing family!

Journal Writing

Date:

Please write three specific attitude of gratitude statements below:

*

*

*

Call to Action

Who will you empower with an attitude of gratitude today?

*

How will you empower _____ with an attitude of gratitude today?

*

6 | ATTITUDE OF GRATITUDE

Specifically, when will you empower
_____with an attitude of gratitude today?

REMEMBER ME

Remember me, dear Lord,
When the clouds fade away
And the sun goes down,
When the sea evaporates
And the grass withers.
Remember me.

Remember my good deeds
And remember your servant's heart.

When the air that we breathe no longer exists,
Remember this.

I love you, Jesus,
You and only you.
No other god, no other idol;
No other being, person, place, or thing more Than you.

Your kingdom
Forever in my heart,
Your praise
Forever on my lips,
Your goodness
Forever on my mind.

Remember me, dear Lord.

In my old age, forget me not.
Keep me, dear Lord.
Just like a baby that needs his mother's milk,
I need your *love*.

I cherish this day
With the thoughts of *you*.
Grant me long life, Lord,
And eternity with *you*.

Throw my sins into the sea of forgetfulness, dear Lord.
Remember not the sins of my youth.
Forgive me, Lord,
Because I am yours.

Remember me.

DAY 2

Fix Your Focus

Jesus

Luke 10:38–42

As Jesus and his disciples were on their way, he came to a village where a woman named Martha opened her home to him. She had a sister called Mary, who sat at the Lord's feet listening to what he said. But Martha was distracted by all the preparations that had to be made. She came to him and asked, "Lord, don't you care that my sister has left me to do the work by myself? Tell her to help me!" "Martha, Martha," the Lord answered, "you are worried and upset about many things, but few things are needed—or indeed only one. Mary has chosen what is better, and it will not be taken away from her."

Coffee

Attitude determines altitude, and this particular Scripture is a perfect testament of this. Instead of Martha having an attitude of gratitude for Jesus's presence, she chose to fuss over what her sister (Mary) was not doing. Despite Martha's frustration, the Bible tells us Mary chose the better option. She expressed an attitude of gratitude while patiently sitting at the feet of Jesus.

Although sitting and listening, Mary's attentive posture to Jesus took more action than Martha. A sincere attitude of gratitude takes action, takes courage. Mary did both. If you have ever been in the same shoes as Martha, busy and hasty about the wrong things, don't feel bad. We've all been busy, moving and shaking to the beat of our own drums at some point, forgetting to stop and smell the roses.

The key to keeping an attitude of gratitude is to simply fix our focus. When we fix our gaze on Jesus, he has a profound way of putting all aspects of our life in place. So the next time this happens, remember that as his children, the Lord promised to give us rest, but we must first sit still and know he is with us, in our presence, every day!

Prayer

> Heavenly Father, I come to you as humbly as I know how, thanking you for all your many blessings—whether big or small. I recognize

that you alone are worthy to be praised, just because of who you are! Enter my heart on this day, Lord. Create in me a new spirit—one filled with joy and peace beyond all understanding. Allow me to reflect on your goodness today and all the days of my life! Forgive me for my mumbling, grumbling, and complaining spirit. I speak life, encouragement, and pure joy over my circumstances, family, friends, and community on this day!

In Jesus's name I ask; in God's name I pray, amen.

Journal Writing

Date:

Please write three specific "attitude of gratitude" statements below:

*

*

*

CALL TO ACTION

Who will you empower with an attitude of gratitude today?

*

How will you empower _____ with an attitude of gratitude today?

*

Specifically, when will you empower _____ with an attitude of gratitude today?

*

JESUS

Joy

> This world didn't give and can't take away,

Embraced

> By your love, redeemed by your

Spirit,

> Unmatched in your grace, no sweeter name do I know—

Savior.

DAY 3

God's perfect timing

Jesus

Lamentations 3:25–26

The Lord is good to those whose hope is in him, to the one who seeks him; it is good to wait quietly for the salvation of the Lord.

Coffee

Growing up in a southern Baptist church, the old folks used to have a saying that still resounds truthfully today. He's an on-time God, yes, he is. He may not come when you want him, but he'll be there right on time!

I remember not fully understanding this concept as a child; I'd ask myself *How can God be on time if he's late at handling my request?* Boy, oh boy, was I naïve. As you live, walk, and grow in your faith with Christ, you'll begin to realize that God is more about your journey than he is about your end result. His divine and perfect knowledge surpasses our understanding.

The Bible tells us in Isaiah 55:8 "'For my thoughts are not your thoughts, neither are your ways my ways,' declares the Lord." Having an attitude of gratitude means rejoicing and praising the Lord while you're waiting for a breakthrough, while you're in the waiting room, when things don't go your way, and most certainly when you come out on the other side clean. Only by his grace and mercy can this be achieved!

I'm reminded of a long business trip taken a few years ago. I had been away from my family all week and was flying from Phoenix to LAX and from LAX to home (Charlotte, North Carolina). I was tired; my mind, body, and soul were ready to relax. Well, of course, my flight from Phoenix was running ridiculously behind schedule. I just knew that I was going to miss my connecting flight in LAX. This was a big deal to me, because the flight was already late in the evening. If I missed the connecting flight, then I was going to be left with only two choices—sleep in the LAX airport all night to await the first morning flight (bummer), or find a hotel in the middle of the night and then come back to the airport to depart for home the next morning (bummer option #2). As God would have it, I mentally panicked for no reason at all. The flight that was running ridiculously late from Phoenix to LAX was the same exact flight that I needed to catch from LAX to Charlotte! Furthermore, I was sitting in the same exact row needed for my Charlotte flight. I was worried for absolutely no reason. God is so good!

So declare victory and rejoice in the Lord's goodness and perfect timing today!

Prayer

> Most gracious and wonderful Father, thank you for loving me despite my shortcomings. Thank you for taking such good care of me and my family daily. Forgive me of my impatience and hasty attitude toward the journey you want me to walk. Right now, in the mighty name of Jesus, I ask you to further open my heart to you.

Allow me to be steadfast in your Word, hopeful for your good and faithful promises, and trusting in you and only you! I recognize that all good and perfect things come from you! Renew in me a spirit of gratefulness, even in the times when it appears I may have less; for I know that with you, Jesus, I am never in lack! I love you, I worship you, and I lift up your name!

In Jesus's name I pray; in God's name I ask, amen.

Journal Writing

Date:

Please write three specific "attitude of gratitude" statements below:

*

*

*

Call to Action

Who will you empower with an attitude of gratitude today?

*

How will you empower _____ with an attitude of gratitude today?

*

Specifically, when will you empower _____ with an attitude of gratitude today?

*

TIME

Time is so very precious.

Thank you, Lord, for sharpening my eyesight to cherish this sweet treasure.

As I sit here, 5 a.m., with my baby boy lying restfully on my tummy,

I smile.

Sleepless nights are rewarded with hugs and kisses from my little one.

This time

I will cherish the day

The Lord has made.

I will rejoice

And be glad in it,

For I know someone, somewhere,

Longs for my sleepless night.

Someone longs to hear that sweet cry in the middle of the night.

Gratitude graces my heart as I embrace this season.

I want to be more like Jesus.

Let me start with my husband and my children.

Let me minister to their souls the goodness of God by showing his goodness through me.

This time, with the time that is different,

I'm going to be different.

This time

Made brand new, a new creation in Christ,

My Lord and Savior.

This time I stop wasting time

And savor the Savior's time.

DAY 4

BE STILL

JESUS

PSALM 46:10

He says, "Be still, and know that I am God; I will be exalted among the nations, I will be exalted in the earth."

Coffee

Chatter, talk, murmuring distractions, thoughtless opinions—these are the thoughts that can invade your mind. You want to do the will of God. You want to be a city upon a hill. You want to be like Jesus, but you just don't know where to start.

You could search for advice from your mother, your father, coworkers, and friends; but what God really wants is for you to seek his face first (Matthews 6:33). He wants you to be still and know that he is God. Instead of the evasive noise, be still and acknowledge the still small voice beaming from within your spirit.

Be grateful in the seemingly slow seasons of your life. These seasons produce the most fruit for future times. An attitude of gratitude is about thanking the Lord your God during the dry seasons, acknowledging his powerful presence, and embracing his love as he orders your steps.

Prayer

> Jesus, I want to thank you for abiding in me as I abide in you. Thank you for covering me with your life-saving blood. Father, help me to remain patient and content as I await to hear a loving word from you. I only want what you want for my life—nothing more, nothing less.

I recognize that you are with me in the midst of my storm, and even when all appears to be silent, I trust you, Father! Thank you for keeping me as you order my steps in your Word! Amen.

Journal Writing

Date:

When you list an attitude of gratitude statement, you are

Please write three specific "attitude of gratitude" statements below:

*

*

*

CALL TO ACTION

Who will you empower with an attitude of gratitude today?

*

How will you empower _____ with an attitude of gratitude today?

*

Specifically, when will you empower _____ with an attitude of gratitude today?

*

USE ME

Use me, Lord.

Every pain has a purpose,

Every disappointment has a destination,

Every setback has a setup for your glory, oh Lord.

Use me.

Let me be your conduit, Lord.

Flow your holy power through me

For your good,

For your glory,

For your use alone.

Use me.

Remove my selfish ambitions,

Remove my own selfish gain,

Remove my impurity,

Replace it with your beauty.

Use me, Lord,

And I will speak of your goodness

All the days of my life.

DAY 5

OUTSHINE PAIN

JESUS

MATTHEW 5:4 ESV

"Blessed are those who mourn, for they shall be comforted."

Coffee

I experienced the loss of a dear colleague recently. We essentially worked together in some capacity for close to ten years.

When I learned of her passing, I was immediately filled with grief, disbelief, and all the emotions surrounding a loss. But the more my flesh wanted to reflect on the sadness of this event, the more my spirit wanted to celebrate—celebrate all the good times, the smiles, the laughter, and the real conversations had between my colleague and I, my friend. You see, my brothers and sisters, having an attitude of gratitude extends far beyond written and verbal anecdotes. An attitude of gratitude will embed itself deep down in your soul, if you let it, over time. With the love and grace of Jesus Christ, an attitude of gratitude will help you overcome some of the greatest obstacles or fears you may face in life. Now, with that being said, am I downplaying the precious life of a loved one or friend? No, but what I am saying is that there is power in perspective, and an attitude of gratitude is that very perspective!

So be encouraged and allow your attitude of gratitude to outshine your pain!

Prayer

> Heavenly Father, thank you for allowing your precious Holy Spirit to engulf my mind, my heart, and my spirit. I recognize

there is a season for everything that occurs within my life. Thank you for my remembrance and reflection on your goodness, even in times of hardship, pain, or grief. Continue to allow my attitude of gratitude for your love, and outshine my pain.

In Jesus's name I pray; in God's name I ask, amen.

Journal Writing

Date:

Please write three specific "attitude of gratitude" statements below:

*

*

*

Call to Action

Who will you empower with an attitude of gratitude today?

*

How will you empower _____ with an attitude of gratitude today?

✫

Specifically, when will you empower _____ with an attitude of gratitude today?

✫

THE BLESSING

Just like a child, you comfort me in your bosom

In your warm and loving, tender embrace.

You soothe my worries and fears when I lay my burdens at your feet.

Am I good enough?

Am I smart enough to deliver your holy Word,

Your precious and perfect Word?

Should it ever escape my unworthy lips?

The truth is, I know that I'm unqualified,

Unqualified to the very world I hope you'll save through the use of me.

But there's beauty, beauty in my brokenness,

Beauty in my weakness,

Because you reign,

Because I am willing,

And because you can do all things but fail.

I succeed in you, Jesus.

Thank you for the bounty.

Thank you for the blessing.

Thank for the gift of speech.

And just like Moses,

When I don't know what to speak,

When I don't know what to say,

Send me Aaron—

Anything to enable your Word to go forth

Through this vessel of mine.

I am forever and ever in awe of you, Lord.

DAY 6

LAST PLACE WINS

JESUS

ESTHER 6:6–11

When Haman entered, the king asked him, "What should be done for the man the king delights to honor?" Now Haman thought to himself, "Who is there that the king would rather honor than me?" have them bring a royal robe the king has worn and a horse the king has ridden, one with a royal crest placed on its head. Then let the robe and horse be entrusted to one of the king's most noble princes. Let them robe the man the king delights to honor, and lead him on the horse through the city streets, proclaiming before him, 'This is what is done for the man the king delights to honor!'" "Go at once," the king commanded Haman. "Get the robe and the horse and do just as you have suggested for Mordecai the Jew, who sits at the king's gate. Do not neglect anything you have recommended." So Haman

> *got the robe and the horse. He robed Mordecai, and led him on horseback through the city streets, proclaiming before him, "This is what is done for the man the king delights to honor!"*

COFFEE

In order to fully glean from this text, you must first understand the dynamic and role of each individual referenced. The king in this Scripture is King Xerxes—King of Persia, ruler of more than one hundred and twenty provinces.

Haman was a man of high honor, proclaimed by the king. "After these events, King Xerxes honored Haman son of Hammedatha, the Agagite, elevating him and giving him a seat of honor higher than that of all the other nobles. All the royal officials at the king's gate knelt down and paid honor to Haman, for the king had commanded this concerning him. But Mordecai would not kneel down or pay him honor" (Esther 3:1–2 NIV). Haman was also very haughty and full of himself.

Mordecai was Ester's Jewish caretaker prior to her becoming the queen (King Xerxes's wife). The Bible tells us that he would not bow down and honor Haman. This infuriated Haman, who then coaxed the king into setting a decree to kill all the Jews. This was Haman's way of showing Mordecai who was boss.

What's the point?

I'm here to encourage you that just because the adversary has counted you out doesn't mean it's over! When God is ready to promote you, elevate you, and take you to the next level, no one can stand in the way! In the case of Mordecai, the man with the highest honor in the land had to honor him. Haman thought the king was referring to him when he asked "What should be done for the man the king delights to honor?" The adversary Haman thought more of himself than he should have, and unbeknownst to himself was advising the king of how he should honor his enemy.

In simpler terms, my friends, *don't worry about your haters*! Your haters can't stop what God has anointed and appointed in *you*! In the kingdom of God, he who is last shall be first!

So, my friends, remember to cast your cares on the Lord and keep an attitude of gratitude concerning the Lord and all his magnificent ways, because he cares for you. He will and can make your enemies your footstool (Luke 20:43). Remember, when you are down to nothing, God is always up to something!

Prayer

> Heavenly and most gracious Father, help me to be more like you with each passing day. Help me to patiently wait for you to reveal your glory to me. Help me to recognize your goodness, whether big and bold or small and

subtle. I give you praise, Father, because of who you are!

Thank you in advance for elevating me to places I have never dreamed of being in. Thank you in advance for enlarging my territory while creating in me the character, humility, and integrity needed to stay there.

And heavenly Father, bless those who wish me ill will. Have grace and mercy on their souls, as they do not realize that what you have blessed cannot be cursed. Thank you for the peace that transcends all understanding in this season of my life! I acknowledge you and know that you are with me. I love you and I thank you!

In Jesus's name I pray; in God's name I ask, amen.

Journal Writing

Date:

Please write three specific "attitude of gratitude" statements below:

*

*

*

CALL TO ACTION

Who will you empower with an attitude of gratitude today?

*

How will you empower _____ with an attitude of gratitude today?

*

Specifically, when will you empower _____ with an attitude of gratitude today?

*

GREATER

You are *greater* than my obstacles,
Greater than my foes,
Greater than my haters,
Greater than my finances,
Greater than my shame,
Greater than my guilt,
Greater than my sin.

You are *greater* than those who conspire against me,
Greater than the naysayers,
Greater than homelessness,
Greater than depression,
Greater than pain,
Greater than loneliness,
Greater than all sickness.

You are *bigger* than any mountain,
Bigger than my frustration,
Bigger than my disappointment,
Bigger than death.
You are the way, the truth, and the life.

You are greater.

Greater you are,

Greater, greater, greater.

DAY 7

SITTING ON A MILLION

JESUS

1 CHRONICLES 17:26–27

> "You, Lord, are God! You have promised these good things to your servant. Now you have been pleased to bless the house of your servant, that it may continue forever in your sight; for you, Lord, have blessed it, and it will be blessed forever."

COFFEE

Everybody loves the lottery. I'm talking megabucks awarded to some deserving or not-so-deserving soul. The chances of winning are rare, but the stakes are too high to pass up for most people. People swarm local gas stations just to get an opportunity of hitting the big jackpot.

Can you imagine winning such a fortune, having the winning ticket, knowing what this change would do for your life, your family's life? Now imagine that you have the winning ticket and you *choose* to refuse to sign it; you never take it to the lottery office to claim your prize, and in essence, you let your ticket— your life-changing winnings—expire? You're probably thinking to yourself, Yeah right, I'd never let that happen! What's the point of that? Sounds foolish, right? Although I'm not advocating playing the lottery, or gambling of any sort, I'd like to paint the imagery of how we, as Christians, sit still on the blessings the Lord has given us. What was the point of Jesus dying on the cross for our sins, giving us access to the Tree of Life, and giving us his grace and mercy if we don't even accept it?

What's the point of receiving God's blessings over our lives if we don't even claim the prize but sit on our blessings until they expire—neglecting the talents and gifts the Lord has given us. These blessings, gifts, and talents given are life altering for you, your family, and those around you. Yet oftentimes we choose to refuse to sign our blessings, put our name on them, and claim them! We allow our blessings, gifts, and talents to expire when we don't use them, when we're not obedient to what God has called us to do, even in the small things. We want more, but we only want to give God less.

Having an attitude of gratitude is more than a catchphrase; it's a living, breathing verb that requires action! The Scripture tells us clearly that we are blessed, but we must be sure to hold firmly to the blessings God has promised us! I challenge you to take hold of your milk and honey. Be reassured that what God has blessed forever will always be blessed forever!

Prayer

> Heavenly Father, I speak generational blessings, love, peace, joy, and prosperity over my life, my family's life, and those in connection through Jesus Christ, my Lord and Savior! I recognize that I am blessed and highly favored, not because I am worthy, but because you alone are worthy.
>
> Right now, in the mighty name of Jesus, I claim, receive, and take hold of the blessings, gifts, and talents you have given me. I no longer question, delay, or refuse the good and perfect gifts you have given to me. From this day forward, I press toward the mark and seek you first in all that I do.

Forgive me, Father, for misusing, abusing, and being wasteful of your love. I trust you, Father, and will acknowledge, proclaim, and grab hold of every good and perfect thing you have called for me to have. I will have an attitude of gratitude for you and your people. I will begin to prove and show it from this day forth. And when I am weak, Father God, and don't know how, what, or where, may I always remember *who*.

In Jesus's name I pray; in God's name I ask, amen.

JOURNAL WRITING

DATE:

Please write three specific "attitude of gratitude" statements below:

*

*

*

Call to Action

Who will you empower with an attitude of gratitude today?

*

How will you empower _____ with an attitude of gratitude today?

*

Specifically, when will you empower _____ with an attitude of gratitude today?

*

LOVE NOTE

Dear God,

You are good, gracious, and merciful to me. Help me, heavenly Father, Yahweh, to understand you better each day, to glean from your wisdom and to be more and more like your son, Jesus Christ, each and every day. Purify my thoughts, dear Lord, so they may reflect upon you, your kingdom, and all things holy, for your glory's sake.

Thank you for loving me in spite of my sins and shortcomings. Thank you for forgiving me and being better to me than I've been to myself! I don't take you or your mighty power for granted. I know that the sun rises and sets because of you. You are the one and only true living God, God of Israel and all the nations before them and after them, and what is to come.

I am your servant and humbly bow down before you, my King! Empower me, teach me, and mold me to preach and teach your wonderful and perfect *will*, Jesus! Allow your Holy Spirit to engulf me and lead me all the days of my life—one hundred and twenty years, to be exact. But most importantly, allow my love for you and your people to grow stronger and stronger every day.

May it be evident in my speech, mannerisms, servitude, attitude, and actions for your kingdom!

I love you, Jesus. Amen.

DAY 8

MESSY PRAISE

JESUS

1 THESSALONIANS 5:16–18

Rejoice always, pray continually, give thanks in all circumstances; for this is God's will for you in Christ Jesus.

Coffee

The alarm goes off, it's 7:30 a.m., and I need to get my daughter up for school while managing to keep my three-month-old son asleep. Epic fail. I cut off the alarm to lie back down for two minutes, which, unbeknownst to me, turns into ten minutes. I quickly make a mad dash to wake my daughter and now the baby's crying. He obviously didn't get the memo (stay asleep while Mommy gets your sister ready for school). With seven minutes to spare, I decide to nurse my little one (this usually puts him back to sleep). First success of the day.

I quickly burp him and lay him down in his bassinet beside his dad, who's on the couch. (Dad is sleeping like a baby, of course.) I grab a t-shirt and my daughter and I scramble out the door just in time to say our morning prayer and help her catch the school bus. I sigh in relief.
Upon entering the home, guess who's up?
My little wiggle bot is awake and he's looking for Mommy. I ask my hubby to hold the baby for a quick second while I wash my hands and put on a pot of coffee (I need a whole lot of Jesus and a little bit of coffee).

I get hold of my little fella, put him in my Babypeta swaddle carrier, and walk him around the house until he's asleep. While taking him on his sleepyland stroll, I notice several things out of whack. Baby bottles on the kitchen table and side table, cups with Pepsi and water left on the dining table, dishes in the sink from last night's supper, hubby on the couch asleep again, daughter's bed unmade, and the list could go on. My first inclination could be to stand over my husband and say it's time to get up and clean up, or How many times do I have to say...? and again, the list could go on and on. But today, the Holy Spirit speaks gently into my heart *An attitude of gratitude. Be grateful, be thankful.*

You see, the massive baby bottle count is from the good Lord giving me an overflow in milk supply to feed my son; the cups on the counter and the dishes in the sink come from the amazing gumbo my husband cooked last night and the special request Pepsi Wild Cherry I asked for. My sleeping husband on the couch comes from a night of Daddy letting Mommy sleep peacefully in our bedroom without the murmurs or requests from our baby. And our daughter's unkempt bed, well, that's just a growing ten-year-old who didn't make up the bed before school. The point I'm making is simple: I'm grateful for our family's quirks, nuances, and imperfections. Our house is lived in and our house represents love. I'm reminded in the Scripture to rejoice always (1 Thessalonians 5:16).

I also recognize that someone, somewhere, longs to have a home-cooked meal by a loving spouse, a sink full of dishes, a child's unmade bed, and baby bottles on the counterspace.

As I continue to challenge myself in the living, breathing Word of God, I also challenge you: Be grateful for the perspectives of life.

The likelihood that someone else is hoping to fill your shoes is great, and the likelihood that someone is waiting to glean from your perspective is greater.

Choose gratitude.

Prayer

> Heavenly Father, I stretch my hand to you, acknowledging that you are good and perfect in all your ways. Thank you for this day, Father. No matter what comes my way, help me to rejoice and be glad in it. Lord, I thank you for my life, my family's life, friends, and those around me you have sent for me to love, honor, respect, and cherish.
>
> Let me not grow weary in the perceived messiness or disorder of my day, because I know that you are with me, guiding me, and leading the way. I love you and thank you for your perfect perspective on this day. Help me to see it like you!
>
> In Jesus's name I pray; in God's name I ask, amen.

Journal Writing

Date:

Please write three specific "attitude of gratitude" statements below:

*

*

*

Call to Action

Who will you empower with an attitude of gratitude today?

*

How will you empower _____ with an attitude of gratitude today?

*

Specifically, when will you empower _____ with an attitude of gratitude today?

*

FLAWS

Forgiven

    By the blood,

Loved

    Despite my mistakes,

Appointed

    By the King,

Winning

    Against all odds,

Saved

    By his grace.

DAY 9

MISSING THE MARK

JESUS

1 CORINTHIANS 9:24

Do you not know that in a race all the runners run, but only one gets the prize? Run in such a way as to get the prize.

Coffee

Have you ever been in such a hurry to reach your mark or destination that you actually miss the entire point? Sounds counterintuitive, I know.

Well, I've definitely been there. And if I'm honest, more times than I care to admit. I was always taught to work hard, finish strong, and soar high. I blame the school system (just kidding). In all actuality, this type of thought process is good, but only as good as the intentions of the doer. The intentions must not only be pure; they must also have a purpose. Otherwise, what's the point?

I recall wanting to make this grand dinner for my family, trying to emulate the "perfect" wife, mother, and home cook. The meal itself wasn't the most important thing, but the purpose was to get validation from my family for an amazing meal, specifically the cornbread. I don't know about you, but down south, we take a few staple food items seriously—fried chicken, potato salad, sweet tea, and cornbread are some of them.

I remember striving to move quickly because, of course, the perfect wife and perfect mom has dinner ready at a perfect time. (Sounds silly, right?) Well, in my pursuit of fast perfection, I proceeded to make the best cornbread ever without a drop of egg. I even went so far as to whip up the clumpy compound. I recognized that it looked strange but proceeded to put it in the oven. Thank goodness the good Lord gave me a lightbulb moment and I finally remembered the egg. I quickly whipped open the oven, got all the mix out of the pan, and added my precious egg. Needless to say, the cornbread was delicious and Mommy saved the day.

So where am I going?

In an effort to quickly cook the perfect meal, I almost missed the key ingredient. It's funny how we can almost miss the mark in our very own spiritual lives. We're going one hundred miles an hour, reading our Bibles, attending Bible study and church—twice on Sundays. We're volunteering at the local soup kitchen and helping the PTA in school…but we're missing the point, continuously missing the mark, when we focus solely on the religion behind our Christianity and forget about our relationship with Jesus.

An attitude of gratitude is all about embracing the journey, the mountaintop highs, the valley lows, and, at times, the inconsistent peaks. An attitude of gratitude is about finding genuine joy and peace for our lives in all of God's splendor. It's about enjoying the slow yet steady pace and space he has created exclusively for you and him. Cherish the intimate setting the Lord creates for you during times of tribulation and triumph. This is the beauty of relationship and not just the façade of religion.

The challenge is this: Find a way to experience relationship with Christ today.

Prayer

Jesus, help me to get to know you better today. Don't allow me to hide behind the busyness of you. Help me to seek an intimate, meaningful, purposeful relationship with you today. I love you, Lord. I worship you and adore your holy name. Now let me act like it and slow down my pace to hear a word from you.

In Jesus's name I pray; in God's name I ask, amen.

Journal Writing

Date:

Please write three specific "attitude of gratitude" statements below:

*

*

*

CALL TO ACTION

Who will you empower with an attitude of gratitude today?

*

How will you empower _____ with an attitude of gratitude today?

*

Specifically, when will you empower _____ with an attitude of gratitude today?

*

THANKS

Heavenly Father,

Thank you for waking me and my family up this morning and for the warm blood running through our veins. Thank you for providing food on the table and a roof over our heads. Thank you for allowing us to sleep and slumber peacefully through the night.

We love you and we thank you for your mercies made new on this day. Father, send your hedge of protection around us as we embark on this day. Father God, enable us to be everything you have called us to be on this day, and nothing of what you have not!

I ask for special healing today, Jesus, over this nation, our leaders, and public officials. Give them the wisdom, discernment, and compassion to do your *will* with integrity, in Spirit and in truth.

Shape the hearts and minds of your clergymen, ministers, evangelists, deacons, volunteers, and members of your church. May they transform the world for your glory.

I prayerfully seek your face for all those hurting right now, Father God! The victims of catastrophic hurricanes, severe earthquakes around the globe; and massive shootings in our country, Jesus!

Only you can heal this broken land, these broken hearts, and your broken people.

I trust in you, Lord.

DAY 10

BETTER OR BITTER

JESUS

JOB 42:10

After Job had prayed for his friends, the Lord restored his fortunes and gave him twice as much as he had before.

Coffee

Have you ever been in a funk? I'm talking about absolutely nothing going your way. Bills are late and the creditors won't give you an extension; your car needs major repair work but your funds are low; you and your spouse are not seeing eye to eye right now; your children have gotten on your last nerve; the doctor report was not the best; and to top it off, your boss has the audacity to put you on the Saturday schedule when she knows you requested that particular weekend off months ago. Have you ever had one of those seasons in your life—where it appears that the sun won't even shine your way? If so, this devotional is for you.

The book of Job is a remarkable testament of endurance for long-suffering. The Bible tells us Job was blameless and upright (Job 1:1); however, he was set to endure hardship after hardship at the prompting of God, himself. He essentially went from being wealthy with a wife, kids, and an abundance of livestock and servants, to destitute, broke, sickly, lonely, and yearning for death to end his misery. Talk about a bad break. Job had it bad and he did right in the eyes of the Lord!

Fact: Part of being a Christian is to be more like Christ—he truly was blameless and without sin, yet he was persecuted, mocked, beaten, spat on, and ultimately crucified for our sins. If we want to walk out our faith, if we want to wave the Christian banner, then we need to know that long-suffering for his name's sake will take place. Not what you wanted to hear, right? I know; Job didn't want to hear it nor experience it either. But God.

In order to grow and be *everything* God has called us to be, we must be tested, we must be pruned, and we must be able to endure a time of trial and tribulation. If we want to take it to the next level in our faith, then we must learn and grow from every season. So what am I saying? Count it all joy! John 15:2 tells us, "He cuts off every branch in me that bears no fruit, while every branch that does bear fruit he prunes so that it will be even more fruitful."

So take solace. The fact that you are still breathing and still standing in his Word, should be proof enough that God wants you to bear more fruit! He wants you to be prosperous, successful, elevated, and winning for his glory! So the next time it seems like you're behind, losing, and defeated, remember this: The good Lord restored Job with double for his trouble, and he can do the same thing for you!

Prayer

> Heavenly Father, you are so amazing, and I thank you for all your wonder and splendor. Bless this day, for you have given me another opportunity to get it right. Father, on this day create in me a spirit of patience and long-suffering like you did for Job. Help me to not despise my pruning season, but

realize the greater work you are doing within me for your glory.

Father, I recognize that your ways are not my ways and your thoughts are much higher than mine. Remind me ever so gently to have an attitude of gratitude, even during my pruning season. I love you and worship your holy name.

In Jesus's name I pray; in God's name I ask, amen.

Journal Writing

Date:

Please write three specific "attitude of gratitude" statements below:

*

*

*

CALL TO ACTION

Who will you empower with an attitude of gratitude today?

*

How will you empower _____ with an attitude of gratitude today?

*

Specifically, when will you empower _____ with an attitude of gratitude today?

*

GRATITUDE

Gratitude—

More than nice,

More than kind,

More than a gesture.

Show your heart,

Show your intent,

Show your character.

Take action,

Move now,

Be blessed,

Bless others.

Do the right thing,

Waste less time,

Be obedient,

Act now.

Fulfill your purpose,

Walk in your destiny

For *his* glory,

Tell your story.

Hold your head high,

Take pride in him alone,

Command your atmosphere.

Avoid temptation,

Rebuke the evil one,

Magnify the Lord.

Show your heart,

Show your intent,

Show your character.

More than nice,

More than kind,

More than a gesture.

Gratitude

DAY 11

IT'S ALL GOOD

JESUS

PSALM 139:14; 2 CORINTHIANS 12:9; 1 SAMUEL 16:7

I praise you because I am fearfully and wonderfully made; your works are wonderful, I know that full well.

But he said to me, "My grace is sufficient for you, for my power is made perfect in weakness." Therefore, I will boast all the more gladly about my weaknesses, so that Christ's power may rest on me.

But the Lord said to Samuel, "Do not consider his appearance or his height, for I have rejected him. The Lord does not look at the things people look at. People look at the outward appearance, but the Lord looks at the heart."

COFFEE

My daughter's school was having a Spirit week (our ten-year-old), and on this particular day, she was to dress up like her favorite book character. This consisted of a raspberry striped dress over jeans, coffee- and tan-colored flats, a cardigan, and her hair pulled into two pigtails.

After our morning prayer, while we waited for the school bus, I asked "What character did you decide?" My daughter quickly told me Nikki from *Dork Diaries*. I asked "Why did you choose her?" She said that Nikki was unpopular in school but she had a good heart, and that's why she chose to be her.

Out of the mouth of babes.

I began to think about how the world will warp our minds, if we let it. The world has a funny way of making us feel less than, marginalized, and beneath. With all the filtered, photoshopped selfies on social media, the rail-thin, airbrushed models on the magazines and billboards, and the constant bombarding of beautiful celebrities, it's no wonder a self-deflating image can be derived. Well, I'm here to tell you, what you see is not always what you get.

Often people's greatest fear is rejection. This overwhelming fear of rejection or not fitting in comes from a false sense of reality. People capture and upload photos of happy days, good times, laughs and giggles to their timeline and newsfeed just for the temporary like, when something much deeper is brewing in their spirit.

Don't get caught up in the trap of comparison.

The Bible tells us we are wonderfully made (Psalm 139:14). Please know that you matter. Every flaw, every mistake, every imperfection is designed to draw us nearer to the cross and Jesus Christ. Know that it is okay to feel weak at times, because the Bible tells us he is made strong in our weakness (2 Corinthians 12:9). When we choose to seek Jesus Christ first, he will fill in all the gaps.

Remember that God seeks a man's heart (1 Samuel 16:7). Outward appearance and superficial, material things mean nothing to the kingdom. Don't get me wrong; they're nice to have, and the Lord will give us the desires of our hearts, but ultimately the tangible "thing" you seek can't get you into heaven, but it could lead to the gateway of hell.

So your attitude of gratitude message is simple here: It's all good. You're all good and perfectly made in the Lord's eyes. You couldn't do one more thing for the Lord to love you any more than he already does. You are a precious jewel, and the Lord only wants you to seek his validation and not that of mortal men. So thank God for today and know that it's all good!

Prayer

Heavenly Father, wow; you are amazing! You are simply amazing and wonderful to me.

I thank you right now, in the mighty name of Jesus, that I don't respond to the people but answer to the call you have over my life! I take pride in you alone and boast in your divine goodness. I believe and receive every good thing you have said over my life!

Help me to be strong and virtuous in you. No matter what the haters say, no matter what the enemy implies, you are more than enough in me! And because of that:

I am good enough.
I am strong enough.
I am smart enough.
I am loved enough.
I am beautiful enough,
And so much more,
Because your grace is sufficient enough for me.

In Jesus's name I pray; in God's name I ask, amen.

Journal Writing

Date:

Please write three specific "attitude of gratitude" statements below:

*

*

*

Call to Action

Who will you empower with an attitude of gratitude today?

*

How will you empower _____ with an attitude of gratitude today?

*

Specifically, when will you empower _____ with an attitude of gratitude today?

*

I AM

Heavenly Father,

Some days I feel weak,

Less than what you made me to be,

Less than what you called me to be,

Tired of striving for perfection.

Dutiful wife, doting mother, minister of faith, best friend to some, acquaintances to most, and role model to all—

Sometimes I feel that I'm not good enough, strong enough, pretty enough, skinny enough, light enough, tall enough, quiet enough, encouraging enough,

And the list could go on and on and on;

But then something beautiful, indescribable happens in my brokenness—

I am made strong!

You remind me in your Word exactly who I *am* and whose I *am*,

And then I smile.

I *am* bold.

I *am* victorious.

I *am* fruitful.

I *am* the branches; Jesus is the vine.

I *am* rich in the Lord.

I *am* blessed and highly favored.

I *am* an overcomer.

I *am* protected by God's angels.

I *am* the head and not the tail.

I *am* above and not beneath.

I am

A child of God,

So

I shall prosper.

I shall bless others.

I shall be the hands and feet of Jesus.

I shall love my husband and respect our marriage.

I shall raise God-fearing and loving children.

I shall be a good neighbor.

I shall feed the poor and visit the sick.

I shall be a good friend.

I shall pray for those who curse me

Because no man can curse what God has blessed.

I *am* and I shall be everything you have called me to be.

As often as I remember you
I will remember this,
In Jesus's name.

DAY 12

IN THE END

JESUS

PSALM 6:2–3

Have mercy on me, Lord, for I am faint; heal me, Lord, for my bones are in agony. My soul is in deep anguish. How long, Lord, how long?

Coffee

The journey we take in this life is not for the faint of heart. Just as a man receives blessings and unmerited favor, he will also receive tests, trials, and tribulations. One thing is for certain—when we choose to be yoked with Christ and abound in his love, what doesn't kill us only makes us stronger through Jesus Christ, who gives us strength.

The Bible gives us plenty of examples of those who overcame perilous dangers and trials. And just like King David, the author of Psalms, we, too, can find our breakthroughs in prayer and praise!

I'm reminded of the sheer strength of my mother. Growing up, we didn't always have what we wanted, but my mother always made sure that we had what we needed. We never missed a birthday and we never missed a meal. I remember watching her get up sometimes before the sun would rise, just so she could stand in a long line at our local assistance agency to receive help with the utility bills. Through God and the support of the community, she kept the lights on. She was never prideful or ashamed. She was humble and trusted in the Lord, even as we endured various hardships. She showed me longsuffering, resilient faith, and how to praise toward your breakthrough! So as I encourage you, I encourage myself to stand firm in his Word and loving embrace.

There is something ever so peaceful and pleasant about knowing who you are and who you belong to, even when the chips are down. So the next time your back seems to be against a wall, the adversary thinks you're all tapped out, and loved ones misunderstand you, remember this: "Surely, Lord, you bless the righteous; you surround them with your favor as with a shield" (Psalm 5:12). God bless.

Prayer

> Heavenly Father, thank you for never leaving my side! Thank you for letting me know that you are with me, even in my darkest hour. I may not understand all the attacks that come my way; I may not understand the path you will have me take; but what I do know is this: I have never seen the righteous forsaken. Thank you, Lord, for allowing me to be a living witness and withstand any trials that may come my way, for your glory!
>
> In Jesus's name I pray; in God's name I ask, amen.

Journal Writing

Date:

Please write three specific "attitude of gratitude" statements below:

82 | ATTITUDE OF GRATITUDE

*

*

*

CALL TO ACTION

Who will you empower with an attitude of gratitude today?

*

How will you empower _____ with an attitude of gratitude today?

*

Specifically, when will you empower _____ with an attitude of gratitude today?

*

YOU WAITED

Dear Jesus,

    You waited for me

When I was deep in sin,

    Lost in the sea that leads to death.

You called my name.

    Condemn me—you did not,

        Rather, you opened your loving arms

            And you showed me grace.

DAY 13

CREATE SPACE

JESUS

MARK 1:35

Very early in the morning, while it was still dark, Jesus got up, left the house and went off to a solitary place, where he prayed.

Coffee

I am often inspired by God in the wee hours of the morning. Maybe this is so because everything is slowed down to a simple sweet crawl. My house is quiet, with the occasional movement of my little guy.

The Lord can speak to us when we sit still long enough to glean from his Word—his will over our lives. In this moment, I am again reminded of God's goodness. I am reminded of his faithfulness. It is well with my soul, no matter what the day brings, because *Jesus* is on my side! And because of that, I have the ability to command my morning, my afternoon, and my evening. I walk, talk, and move fully knowing I can complete every good task he has called me to. He has equipped me. I may stumble because I am not perfect, but with the Lord on my side, I won't fall because *he is!*

My challenge to you is this: Where can you go? What place has God created for you to dwell in him freely, quietly, and with minimal interruption? Now go. Acknowledge the moment in this precious capsule of time designated just for you and Jesus. Live in that moment, reflect on his goodness, pray to him, adore him. Just flat out talk to him. He hears you and welcomes your desire to engage in an intimate time with him—the Creator of all things! Be blessed and be a blessing.

Prayer

Heavenly Father, open my heart and open my mind to hear a word from you today! Help me recognize the space you've created for me to seek your face. Let me be deliberate and intentional in every encounter with you, when in need and when in *love*.

In Jesus's name I pray; in God's name I ask, amen.

Journal Writing

Date:

Please write three specific "attitude of gratitude" statements below:

*

*

*

Call to Action

Who will you empower with an attitude of gratitude today?

*

How will you empower _____ with an attitude of gratitude today?

*

Specifically, when will you empower _____ with an attitude of gratitude today?

*

LOVE NOTES TO JESUS

So grateful to God for the opportunity to do his *will*.

He is so amazing.

So glad Jesus makes provision for me

And

Grants me his perspective,

Orders my steps and dispatches his angels to go before me

to foreign and familiar places.

Oh, the places I will go with Jesus!

He gives me words to say when I am speechless, and living water to drink when

I am thirsty.

He feeds my spirit and nourishes my soul with his prophetic word

And gives me thoughts to make things happen

According to his *will!*

He is the reason Mona was Lisa

and Picasso's paintings are revered.

He's the reason the sun shines and the wolf howls at the moon,

The reason the wind blows and the river floats downstream,

The reason we smile,

The reason we breathe the air that we breathe,

And the reason behind a newborn baby's coo.

Mountains move in the presence of his greatness

And the earth quakes under his almighty power!

He is beauty personified,

And no sweeter name do I know than

Jesus!

I love you, I thank you,

I adore you, Father.

Allow me to be pleasing in your sight.

Allow your love to *shine* through me.

Allow me to be the hands and feet of *you*, Jesus.

I love you, I thank you,

I adore you, Father!

You are indescribable, magnificent,

And worthy to be praised.

Remain on my mind as often as a newborn baby bird chirps for food.

Flutter in my heart more often than a butterfly flaps its wings in the spring.

Let me hum a hymn of praise as frequently as a hummingbird sings a song when the flowers bloom.

Allow me to manifest your words day and night.

Your words becoming my words, and my words becoming your *will* for my life!

Let the sinful ways of my flesh die daily,

And your living Holy Spirit

Be resurrected within me daily.

Make me a new creature

In Christ daily—

Stronger, wiser, kinder, humbler, and lovelier

Than the day before,

In Jesus's sight

And for his glory alone.

Purify my heart, oh gracious, kind, and wonderful creator of the universe.

Jesus,

I love you, I thank you,

and I adore you, oh heavenly Father

Because you first loved me,

Your servant,

Your child,

Nakita

DAY 14

WAIT IN HOPE

JESUS

PSALM 33:20

We wait in hope for the Lord; he is our help and our shield.

COFFEE

Have you ever been waiting for something or someone to move, make a change, or acknowledge what you need or deserve? Waiting, in itself, can be a brain eater. In other words, waiting for the next promotion, waiting for that next paycheck, waiting for him or her to do right, and just plain waiting in general has the ability of producing two completely different emotions—anxiety, if we so choose, or hope! It's all about perspective.

In all transparency, I've recalled feeling a spirit of anxiety while in the waiting room. I've also experienced the feeling of hope brightly shining in my soul. I can tell you, with a firm grasp of both, that the latter of the two is more peaceful and pleasing. "For God hath not given us the spirit of fear; but of power, and of love, and of a sound mind" (2 Timothy 1:7 KJV).

When we choose to wait in hope, we choose to exercise our faith. We remain hopeful, expecting God's goodness to show up and show out on our behalf in his divine appointed time. The waiting room has built strong faith and a firm foundation for greatness for those who choose to wait in the hope found in Jesus Christ!

Don't believe me? Just ask Abraham, who waited in hope until he was one hundred years old to receive his promise of offspring, his Isaac. Just ask David, who waited in hope as he tended to his family's sheep patiently before he was anointed, and even longer before he officially became king. Just ask Ruth, who chose to wait in hope despite her mother-in-law waiting in anxiety. Ruth diligently and patiently gleaned the fields before being wedded to the wealthy Boaz. Waiting in hope ultimately led her to be in the direct lineage of Jesus! The moral of the story is simple: Choose to wait in hope, no matter the circumstances, and the Lord will pour out a blessing bigger than you even know how to receive. Trust in him!

PRAYER

Heavenly Father, you are amazing, awe inspiring, and worthy to be praised! Every good thing I have or ever will be, is because of you. Help me, Lord, on this day to please you with my faith and hope in you. Remove all self-doubt and worry on this day. Help me to acknowledge that you are fighting for me and with me in all my battles, seen and unseen. You are my refuge and my fortress. Thank you for loving me the way you do!

In Jesus's name I pray; in God's name I ask, amen.

Journal Writing

Date:

Please write three specific "attitude of gratitude" statements below:

*

*

*

Call to Action

Who will you empower with an attitude of gratitude today?

*

How will you empower _____ with an attitude of gratitude today?

*

Specifically, when will you empower _____ with an attitude of gratitude today?

*

Afterword

Well, my friend, my brother or sister in Christ, you've done it! If you're reading this text, then you have successfully planted the seed of gratitude in your heart. My hope is that you feel restored, renewed, and revived on this journey we call life. I also hope that you smiled at the Lord's word, gleaned some fresh perspective, and enjoyed a few cups of coffee along the way—I sure did (chuckle). And now my heart rejoices with you as you take real, tangible steps to show an attitude of gratitude, because even the best of us can feel trapped in the day-to-day grind and lose the spirit of gratefulness. As we depart for now, I'll leave you with this:

Gratitude is never silent. King David said it best: "I proclaim your saving acts in the great assembly; I do not seal my lips, Lord, as you know. I do not hide your righteousness in my heart; I speak of your faithfulness and your saving help. I do not conceal your love and your faithfulness from the great assembly" (Psalm 40:9-10).

May the peace and love of Jesus Christ rest, rule, and abide with you for all eternity. In Jesus's name, amen.

Love,

Nakita

Acknowledgments

Thanks be to Jesus Christ, the head of my life and my Lord and Savior! He is my *source* and my *strength*.

Here on earth, I must thank the love of my life, best friend, and compassionate husband—Demecho M. Davis! You love me like a fat kid loves cake (laughs). Your love and support, specifically as I have worked on this book, has been invaluable. You are a blessing to me in every facet, and I can't imagine life without you. So eat your Wheaties,™ kiddo, because you are stuck with me for the next eighty to ninety years! But seriously, you love me like Christ loves the church. You are a shining example of God's love and grace for me. I love you, Papi!

I'd also like to go on record for thanking my beautiful children, Imani and Demecho E., for just being who you are in every stage of your lives. You have blessed my heart so. I am a better person because of the two of you. Remember, Mommy will always love you both and Jesus is the source of your strength! Follow your dreams.

Thanks are in order to my dad, Harold Williams, and my mother-in-law, Janice Davis. You two have been "Johnny on the spot," so selfless, supportive, and loving while my husband and I have been following the calling God has placed over our lives! I pray that God blesses you both with long life, richness in your hearts that money can't buy, and abundance here on earth as in heaven. I am grateful for you—more than you will ever know. I love you.

To my sister Tomeka: God has a calling over your life and a testimony of praise for you to tell. You are bold, beautiful, and more blessed than you know! I love you and speak blessings over your life!

Daphne Mason, Toya Good, and Norma Reeves, this journey we call life wouldn't be the same without you! We may not talk every day, but when we do, it's like we never skipped a beat!

Evangelist Abigail Moats, sister, you are on *fire* for the Lord. Your walk with Christ, prophetic words, and desire to edify God's people has blessed my heart dearly. Thank you for sharing your gifts, support, and encouragement.

Thank you, Sister Ruthene Reddick, for capturing the essence of my gratitude through your cover photo!

If I missed your name, please charge it to my head and not my heart. I love you, and may God bless you all in Jesus's name. Amen.

ABOUT THE AUTHOR

Nakita Davis is an independent ordained minister through the National Association of Christian Ministers. In her pursuit to spread the gospel, Minister Davis has been afforded multiple opportunities to edify, encourage, and inspire others to build a relationship, not a religion, with Jesus Christ.

In 2016 and 2017, Minister Davis was recognized by President Barack Obama for the President's Volunteer Service Award—an elite volunteer program promoting individuals to live a life of servitude through presidential gratitude and national appreciation.

When not ministering to others or serving in her local home church—Elevation—Nakita and her family can be found promoting their Christian apparel line—BelykeChrist (BelykeChrist.com) and Meeko's (her husband's) latest Christian rap album entitled *The Gospel*.

Minister Davis believes that a posture of gratitude is required for the advancement of the gospel, and she uses every platform the Lord gives to inspire the hope, grace, and salvation found in Jesus Christ's love.

Minister Davis and her husband have two beautiful children who reside with them in their Charlotte, NC, home.

CONTACT MINISTER NAKITA DAVIS

WEBSITE: www.jesuscoffeeandprayer.com

FACEBOOK: facebook.com/jesuscoffeeandprayer

INSTAGRAM: instagram.com/jesuscoffeeandprayer

TWITTER: twitter.com/jesuscoffeeandpray

E-MAIL: jesuscoffeeandprayer@gmail.com

A MOMENT WITH THE AUTHOR

PURPOSEFULLY PAINFUL

In the summer of 2008, my heart was ripped right out of my chest, literally. The pain that inflamed my heart burned like a forest fire and cut like a knife.

I remember it like it was yesterday. I was at work when I received a phone call that would change the trajectory of my life. My beloved mother had passed out in a neighboring parking lot while aiding one of her patients. And no, my mother wasn't a nurse, but she was a servant of the Lord. On that particular day, she was taking one of her patients to crisis assistance ministry.

Upon arrival at our local hospital, my mother was unresponsive and in a coma. Within three days of hospitalization, she was taken off life support and pronounced dead.

At the age of eleven, my biological father passed away and now at the age of twenty-three, my mother—my rock, my hero—was gone too. To make matters more complicated, I had just given birth to my first child nine months prior.

I felt alone and angry, yet I still felt an overwhelming sense of responsibility to be strong for everybody else.

But who was going to be strong for me?

For years I played the blame game in my mind. If I were righteous enough, if I'd prayed more, if I'd had enough faith, if I had…if they…if-if-if.

I wish I could tell you that after her passing I immediately knew the importance of life, knew my purpose, and was walking gracefully in it. But I wasn't. I spiraled out of control, focusing only on my career, money, validation of man, and anything that had me as the center of focus. I knew *of* Jesus, but I didn't fully know him for myself. Sure, I had been saved in my youth and baptized in the holy water, but without the guiding hand of my mother, I went astray. Time and time again, I praised the Lord with my mouth but distanced myself by sin.

Sin entangles, you know.

But God.

Then along the way, the Lord sent me someone who cared enough to help me seek his face first.

He invited me to church.

A simple invite followed by kind actions course corrected me back into my Father's flock over time. Soon I began to serve in the local church, tithe faithfully, and rededicate my life to Christ.

The Lord needed me to know he was my rock, he was my refuge, and he was my provider. He needed me to humble myself before his mighty hand and to surrender all. The Lord used my mother to plant the seed of Christ in my life, and for that, I am forever grateful.

Although I miss my mother immensely, I stand before you now with an attitude of gratitude. Without the pain, without the pruning, and without God's grace, I wouldn't have made it this far. The devil wanted to count me out, but Jesus had already counted me in!

The calling has always been placed over my life; I just finally chose to be obedient and answer.

I am living proof. When you give God your pain, he will, in return, give you your purpose!

God bless,
    Nakita

Sneak Peek Book Sequel

Everybody Wants a Piece of Mommy

Attitude of Gratitude Series

How to maintain an attitude of gratitude when your time, energy, and money are stretched thin.

DAY 1

SOFTENED HEART

GENESIS 18:14

"Is anything too hard for the Lord? I will return to you at the appointed time next year, and Sarah will have a son."

Perspective

Once upon a time, I knew a person who wanted nothing more than to have a child. All his friends and family had kids. Everywhere he looked, people were popping out kids left and right, it seemed. He saw people who didn't want kids, abused kids, and neglected kids all over the TV screen. It just seemed so unfair.

He felt his prayers to God were being unanswered. So he finally made up his mind. He thought *It's just not for me to have my own biological child, with my own flesh and blood, my own DNA.* After years of disappointment, prayers, and doing what he felt was right by the Lord, he gave up.

But not the way you may think. He gave up worrying and being frustrated about his situation. He laid his burden down to Jesus and completely focused on him—praising him and thanking him for the life he lived. Then something miraculous happened. God softened the heart of his spouse, and together the two decided to let God's *will* be done regarding a child.

Within two months of truly surrendering all to God, this couple conceived their very first son. That man who remained steadfast and with a heart of gratitude, despite his feelings, was my husband, Demecho Davis. And that woman God softened was me!

We often want God to give us what we want, when we want it, how we want. We want him to overcome our situation suddenly. And although we serve a mighty God, who can do all things but fail, sometimes it's more important for him to take us through the journey than to bring us to the end result. The gap between our expectations and what actually happens is where God wants to stretch us, grow our faith, and increase our praise for his glory! When we finally show the genuine and sincere attitude of gratitude despite the letdowns, despite our trials, despite the heartache and pain—that's where the miraculous begins. I am a living witness.

So begin to have an attitude of gratitude that surpasses all understanding! Confuse the enemy with your praise and watch the God of peace soon crush Satan under your feet (Romans 16:20).

Prayer

> Heavenly Father, thank you for your glory and splendor. Thank you for standing outside of time and knowing exactly what I need and when I need it, before I need it. Forgive me, Lord, for wanting my will to be done instead of yours. You are the Alpha and Omega, author and finisher, the perfecter of my faith. Just like a child, at times I grow impatient and find myself getting ahead of your blessings. Help me to be patient, patiently waiting on your every whim and word for my life. You know what's best for me! Keep me in perfect peace

as I continue this journey we call life. Help me to maintain an attitude of gratitude even when things don't go my way.

I love you, Lord, and know that your Word is true. Your promises never fail, and I will trust you all the way.

In Jesus's name I pray; in God's name I ask, amen.

DAY 2

COMPARISON GAME

JEREMIAH 29:11

"For I know the plans I have for you," declares the LORD, "plans to prosper you and not to harm you, plans to give you hope and a future."

Perspective

My ten-year-old tried out for her school's coed basketball team. She practiced prior to tryouts and really wanted to make the team.
Unfortunately, this year just wasn't her year to play with the school. Although disappointed, she remained resilient with high hopes.

Well a few days later, she was invited to join the National Beta Club because of her scholastics and positive leadership within the school. Awesome, right? Of course, but what was she thinking on the inside? I found out the answer to this question en route to dropping her off at her first Beta Club meeting. It went something like this:

> Daughter: Mom, I wonder how Sally is able to be in the science club, the book club, the soccer team, and now the Beta team with me, all while keeping her grades up?
> Me: Well, baby, that's great for her! God is good. You are happy for her, right?
> Daughter: Yes.
> Me: Different people can handle different things. Don't be concerned, because you will have every good thing that God wants you to have! [Notice that I didn't say she would have everything she wanted, *but* every good thing God wanted her to have!] Amen.
> Daughter: Amen (smiling)

Now, I know what you're saying. That's a great story and all, but how does that apply to me? My issues and fancy adult business is far more important than a child's. Well, I can assist you with that. I can only imagine in our Father's eyes (Jesus's), how we, too, seem to be like children. If we don't get the promotion, the marriage proposal we were expecting (ladies), the raise on the job, or when we feel that Mary has it going on while we barely struggle to get by, I envision the good Lord saying, *You will have every good thing I want for you when you abide in me!*

You see, my sisters (brothers too), comparison has no real value when you are striving to live an attitude of gratitude. Comparison is a trick of the enemy to convince you that you are living in lack—the land of not enough. The reality is God has given us all our very own assignments. The Bible tells us in 1 Corinthians 12:4–6, "There are different kinds of gifts, but the same Spirit distributes them. There are different kinds of service, but the same Lord. There are different kinds of working, but in all of them and in everyone it is the same God at work."

Simply put, stay in your lane and ask the Holy Spirit to guide you on *your* assignment—not your neighbor's, not your coworkers, not your siblings or friends. When we are proven faithful with just a few things, the good Lord will be sure to elevate each of our platforms for his glory!

Prayer

Heavenly Father, thank you for every good spiritual gift you have given me! I count it all joy and know you have plans for me to prosper, because you said it in your Word. Help me, dear Lord, to not grow weary or to move hastily. Allow me to recognize each season and each moment in time that you have perfected just for me. Forgive me, Lord, for every complaint, every murmur, every attitude against your *will* for my life. Create in me a clean and pure spirit, humble and meek for you, yet bold in proclaiming your goodness to the world. I pray, in this moment, for wisdom and discernment so I may know what your perfect and pleasing *will* is for my life.

Heavenly Father, be so kind as to remove any form of hate, envy, or jealousy from my heart. As I pray for myself, I pray for your goodness to fall fresh on my neighbors, my community, and my sisters and brothers in Christ. Heavenly Father, I even pray for those who despise me and boast in themselves. Transform their hearts for your glory, dear Lord.

I love you, Lord, and know that all things are working for my good.

In Jesus's name I pray; in God's name I ask, amen.

Made in the USA
Lexington, KY
02 April 2019